CONSEQ...ES

CONSEQUENCES

U. A. Fanthorpe

PETERLOO POETS

First published in 2000
by Peterloo Poets
The Old Chapel, Sand Lane, Calstock, Cornwall PL18 9QX, U.K.

**A catalogue record for this book is available
from the British Library**

ISBN 1-871471-83-4

Printed in Great Britain by
Antony Rowe Ltd, Eastbourne.

ACKNOWLEDGEMENTS

Acknowledgements are due to the following: *Acumen*; *Atlanta Review* (USA); BBC World Service; Curlew Productions; *Edgeways*; Fat Chance Productions (HTV); *'If the Lord don't come, He d'send'*; *Last Words*; *Orbis*; *A Paean for Peter Porter*; *Picture Poems*; *Plowshares* (USA); *Poetry Ireland*; *Poetry Review*; *Prospero*; *Rive Gauche*; *Seam*; *Soundings*; *Staple*; *Stride*; *Writers' News*.

'Seven Types of Shadow' was commissioned as part of *Ghosts* by the Literature department of the Royal Festival Hall.

Consequences was begun at Hawthornden Castle, worked on at Lumb Bank, and finished at Tŷ Newydd. I am profoundly grateful to Drue Heinz and all at Hawthornden Castle; Amanda Dalton and David Groves of Lumb Bank; and Sally Baker of Tŷ Newydd, who so kindly left me to get on with the job.

One takes public libraries for granted. But most particular thanks are due to Penny Thompson, of Wotton-under-Edge Library, and to Jo Major, now of Minchinhampton Library, for taking so much trouble on my behalf.

In particular, thanks to The Royal Literary Fund, whose generosity has made all the difference.

Thank you, too, to the dear friends who walked with me every step of the way: Diana, Eddie and Di, Polly.

For Rosemarie Bailey
and in happy memory of
Lynn Chambers

Contents

Consequences (A Note)

This sequence is about, among other things, England and Leicestershire and Richard III, and hope, courage and gypsies. It also touches upon war and peace, second sight, and the arms trade, and the uses of language and architecture; and, being late twentieth century, it acknowledges the part played by money in determining what is important. Shakespeare, George Fox, Richard III, Torrigiano, the Master of the Cast Shadow and Urania Boswell all have something to say on these topics. The title (the name of an old party-game) suggests that nothing happens in isolation from the past or the future. *U.A.F.*

Consequences

1. FOUND ON THE BATTLEFIELD

The moorhen slips into the water
Like a Neanderthal bird. And water
Spreads out in planes all over England.

The heiress sits in the manor garden
With her high plucked forehead and her noble bones
Thinking, will it be King Dick or King Harry
That fathers my dynasty?

The precious things, the crowns and golden chains,
Are dirtied, and the fine steel basinets
Rot in the caked and scummy ditches.
Toilet-paper standards flutter from the banks.

This landscape is not given to forgetting.

The moorhen, crabwise and odd as a man-at-arms,
Jerks in the water. A horse shouts in the night,
And a dog finds something beastly to eat
Under a hawthorn. Swans cruise, freighted with meaning,
Eloquent and ferocious as heraldry.
Their painted scowls outstare the afternoon.

It is the usual battlefield, with a hill, a wood,
A marsh, phlegmatic cows, visitors' car park,
Disused railway, battle trails. And people,
No doubt with other things on their minds.

The canal has invaded this landscape,
But it speaks the same idiom: will it be
King Dick or King Harry? Theme park or business centre?
Choose, England.

2. LOST AND LOST

Under the great gold saltcellar, the gilded moorhen
Lost for five hundred years. Lost,
Mourn the archivists, the keepers, the metal detectors.

But maybe not. Perhaps, in its own time,
It will surface. Return and delight, with its pearls
And precious stones, marvellous rich.

But Richard the King is lost for ever,
Under the weight of Leicester City Centre.
Above him trolleys, buggies, perform

Their daily quickstep. Above him workmen
Pitch and toss crates, mothers hurry and go
With cars full of kids and plastic carrier bags.

What mortal bones could resurrect from here?

Richard is lost, and his reputation.
Here lies the bunch-back'd toad, the bottled spider,
The hellhound, the abortive rooting hog,
God's enemy, and England's bloody scourge.

Fine language is one way of being remembered.
This is the best we have. This is Shakespeare.

3. THE MASTER OF THE CAST SHADOW

Some painters leave shadow out. The Master hunts it
From the source of light to where the last
Faint filigree fingertip falls,
Unthinking as a sundial.

We each inherit our shadow, our ration of darkness,
That shrivels and spreads as light walks here and there.

They don't see us, these sad mediaeval faces,
With their crosses, their rings, their daggers, their painted eyes.
They're on the watch for various ugly kinds
Of early death.
                          What they see is the weather,
For the weather warred over England,
As the roses slugged it out: fog at Barnet,
Snow at Towton, three suns at Mortimer's Cross
In the open fighting season. Red Gutters
And Bloody Meadows are sprayed over counties.
They killed and killed and killed. Thirty thousand
In a morning. Where did they find the people?
So few around, so many of them butchered.
But some live on as the Master saw them,
Praying, or holding a naked broken sword.

4. THE YOUNG PERSON'S GUIDE TO ARMS

i   Enemies come in pairs, like socks. There is no such thing as a single enemy.

ii When one enemy kills the other it is called Ethnic Cleansing. Of course, Cleanliness is next to Godliness; and much easier.

iii An Eye For An Eye. This is a very old wargame called Retaliation. However, no one has yet worked out what to do with someone else's Eye.

iv Collateral Damage. This is when Children and Ordinary People come between enemies and get killed. It's really their fault for being in the wrong place at the wrong time.

v   Surgical Strike. This is when you hit One Special Thing, like a surgeon cutting out a cancer. 'Surgical' makes it clear that killing is a good thing.

vi Concentration Camp. Everyone enjoys camping holidays, so people don't worry about what will happen. When you've put the people all together in a Camp, it's much easier to kill them.

vii Liquidate. Another way of getting rid of people. It sounds like making soup, so no one minds.

viii Friendly Fire. This means killing someone on your own side by mistake. Since it saves them from being killed by an enemy, it's quite kind, really.

ix Human Shield. This is when you are very polite, and say 'After you' to women and children and people like that. Then, if your enemy kills them because they're in front of you and in the way, this gives you something called The Moral High Ground.

x   Enemies never forget the past, because it justifies what they are doing. They seldom mention the future, since there might not be any.

5.   HOMILY OF THE HASSOCKS

In Leicestershire, in Sutton Cheney,
in the church where he prayed when time ran out,
not the man himself, but woolly whispers:
Remember before God Richard, remember
and those who fell ... The whisper of hassocks
(gift of The Richard Society). This patient cross-stitch
is done for love not money, in a homely idiom.
Remember before God all the obliterated,
in Sutton Cheney, in Leicestershire,
all the world over, ever.

6.   HATS OFF, GENTLEMEN. A GENIUS!

No. I not like the place. I detest.
What I find here to admire? I,
Artist and citizen of Firenze?

The stink of dirty beards, broccoli,
Herring, bad teeth. A celery language,
Language for ape, not man.

They not comprehend *me*, these idiot workmen,
To whom I am coming like saviour
To world-without-end their little dead English king.

I make the Pope his saints. English Henry? No trouble.
He look like Pope when I finish him,
Though nasty piece of work in life, no doubt.

These English oafs! Cut rope, spill colour,
Crack stone. *The usual accidents, signor,* they smirk.
I comprehend *them*. And I have reputation.

Who fight for Borgia? Stuff Michelangelo
Nasty nose down filthy throat like biscuit?
True, I am exile here, among the beasts,

But money, money, lotsa money! And I make
Effigy to move the heart. *Prodigioso –*
Ma doloroso! These English they so halfwit,
Too greedy to know to praise me good.

7. THE USES OF ARCHITECTURE

'For Ruskin, the hanging fan vaulting in Henry VII's chapel (1502)
was a great sham because it disguised the function of the roof
supports.' (Victor Sage)

When in disgrace with fortune and men's eyes

Distract public attention. A building puts things right.
After the massacre, a hospital
(Sports centre, university),
Anything eye-catching; red herring in stone.

Henry the tax-gatherer, Henry
Reviser of records of all the days before yesterday,
Henry who picked off all heirs but his own,

Lies here in his Henry chapel, named in his name,
In an hysteria of greyhounds and roses,
Portcullises and little red Welsh dragons,
Gilt bronze on black, cherubs at every corner,
Under a ceiling exploding with pendants and putti,
Vaulted like the hand of God. A good buy.

Don't miss that meagre, brooding head. Holy,
You'd say. Ascetic. The best buy of the lot.
Florence's best, of the best period. Torrigiano.
(Never saw Henry, of course, but knew what was wanted:
The austere look. The best, if you can afford it.)
He charged a mint. Worth ever penny, though.

Here's Henry, in a golden web of grace,
For whom the cherubim continually do cry,
And tourists edge past, wanting to get on
To Mary Queen of Scots and Bloody Mary,
But the guide thinks they oughta see this geezer, and somewhere
Out there Richard, under the trolleys, the buggies,
The lamentation of traffic

Remember before God all the obliterated.

8.   MASTER SHAKESPEARE: HIS MAGGOT

(for Brian Vickers)

'I may do that I shall be sorry for.' (*Julius Caesar*)

Not really a good beginning. I like
An uneasy scurrying, *what country's this? who's there?*
With luck, they're hooked.
                              A solo confident voice
Telling us what he'll do before he does it?
Obvious. Obvious.

All Marlowe's doing. Burbage sees himself
As Jew or Faustus, witty, aspiring, perverse,
Poetic justice waiting in Act Five.

But reconciliation's more my line,
And a decent quota of clothcaps talking prose.

Villains are difficult. I haven't the knack.
Circumscribed citizens, without that other dimension
Of unexpectedness, something irregular.
The fans don't fancy moral cloudiness.
They like to know where they are with the criminal classes.

The future nibbles, too. Not just Burbage,
But unborn ghosts of players, Burbages to be,
Wanting this part. *Your hunchback, Will,*
They twitter. *The monster part. The hog! The hog!*

Simplifications of the acting trade:
Crook back, frozen arm, unfinished look.
Hard to refuse the future. Not much choice,
Either, with Burbage at me, moaning about the takings.

I hate predictability. Richard's a Jack-in-the-box
With his *Here we are again.* Jacks are predictable
In their Jackish way. The best bits are
The sudden, sideways turns —
This is All Souls' day, fellow, is it not?

And *They about cockshut time, from troop to troop*
Went through the army cheering up the soldiers.
Something might come of that.

I must do better. No more truck
With scapegoats, Burbage, Marlowe, groundlings,
Actors to come; and you, poor ghost,
Crippled in memory as maimed in life —
Guilt and responsibility; I know about them.

—

9. ASK A SILLY QUESTION

'The age of chivalry is gone. That of sophisters, economists and calculators
has succeeded.'   (Burke, *Reflections on the Revolution in France*)

King Dick or King Harry? Theme park or business centre?
Choose, England.

I choose peace; I never get it.
Takeovers and overtakers, de-militarised zones,
Kings dead in ditches, displaced persons,
Class war, sex war, civil war, war. Tortures,
And other irregularities.
                                        Somewhere, all the time,
A dog is finding something beastly to eat
Under a hawthorn. Does it matter
Who it is, Harry or Dick?
What matters is that people live
The ordinary all-in-a-day's-work life of peace.

They've thought up a disinfected vocabulary
In Rwanda, Lebanon, Bosnia, Ireland, here.
I know the anodyne lexicon: Ethnic Cleansing,
Military Option, Defence Procurement, Friendly Fire –
Language of arms dealers to shareholders
At a safe distance. With a nice feeling
For euphemisms, you can get away with murder.

This was the battlefield. Birds, hedges, sheep,
And long November shadows. *Hedge laying*
On Saturday. Strong clothes, please,
And bring a packed lunch. Remember,
This is a haven for wildlife, with a variety
Of wild flowers and different species
Of butterflies. Please do not pick or harm.

Far off, the inveterate voice of battle:

Who's 'im, Bill?
— A stranger.
'Eave 'alf a brick at 'im.

This is all there is.
No Andes, no Outback. There's no more than this,
And the sea chews away at Suffolk.

10. HUNDREDS AND THOUSANDS

(at Brinklow)

The seesaw rattle of goods trains in the night
Watery quiet observations of duck
The moorhen's morning gurgle

This century excels at calculation
Thirty-five hundred thousand at Dresden,
Seventy-eight hundred thousand at Hiroshima,
The first hundred thousand, the second hundred thousand,
Eight hundred thousand starved at Stalingrad,
Six million in the camps. And other,
Less famous headcounts. This is an age
In serious debt to statistics.
                              One death
Is enough to convince. We don't need crowds
To remind us how precious we all of us are.
Marvellous rich. An offer not to be repeated.

11. FOX UNEARTHED

(for Nick Large)

He is eleven. God is after him.
But what's it mean? What's he supposed to do?

Nineteen now. He ditches job and home.
Hears God saying *Thou must be*
A stranger with all.

          Takes to walking,
A Baedeker journey, from Drayton-in-the-Clay
(Which is the beginning) to Bosworth, Barnet,
Lutterworth, Leicester, through
The muddy muddled middle of Middle England,
Through a world turned upside down.

Where's ta going, George?
God knows.

Thrashing it out with any who seem
To know an answer. Sad adolescent dropout
Unable to settle. Marriage? *Ah no,*
I am but a lad. Not how God sees him.

Treading the water lanes, mouth stuffed with silence,
Eyes re-reading a not-yet-written book,
His shoes in pieces again.

          He hears
What was coming, always. Now it comes:
All things were new, and all the creation
Gave another smell unto me than before.
The smell of God.

Now he can run up the length of England,
To Pendle Hill, the bare unfriendly ridge.

Up wi' thee, George, says God. And being up,
He saw the Lancashire sea, and God's people,
Waiting to be found. So shins up further Firbank,
Drinks water, preaches to a thousand. The beginning
Of the beginning.
      The high moments
On the high places. Fox runs free.

But Fox also trapped in the prisons of England,
Carlisle, Derby, Lancaster, Launceston, Leicester,
Nottingham, Scarborough, Worcester,
In the dark, the cold, the wet, alone.

This is where the chase leads, to the stopped earths
As well as the fell tops. And, dying,
After so much cross-country work, in London, telling friends
I am glad I was here.
      The smell of God
In the muddy, the high, the beastly places.

12. THE FORTUNE-TELLER'S FUNERAL

The seeing has been my life. Handed down
Like silver. No use here, in Farnborough,
Where they know my proper name. But Easter-time
Sees me off on my way to Margate.
A good place to mystify. Westgate sometimes,
Or Broadstairs. All gainful addresses.

Vardo, curtains, crystal ball –
They draw the people. I'd do better in the sun,
In my big chair, holding damp gorgio hands,
Say just as true a future. But they need hocus-pocus,
The lamp, reflections, shadows, me in pearlies,
Queen Gypsy Rose Lee on the posters.

I find the future. They giggle and stare,
Helpless at belief. I muzzle what I know:
How many young women will marry twice,
How many lads die young, in sand or air.
I speak riddles: *Many will love you.*
Beware of high places, of fire and steel.
They can unravel it if they like.

My own death's different. I've planned it.
Picked my undertaker, Mister Owen,
Who did so well by Levi. The procession,
He'll see to it: six jet horses
(My Levi's pals should find a proper match),
Outrider, coachman, flowers and flowers and flowers,
Great wreath in the shape of my special chair,
Romanies walking, three hundred or so,
　　Twenty thousand, I say, twenty thousand
Some in mourning, some not
　　Black triangles, the gypsy Z
　　They are marched through. The see-saw rattle
　　Of goods trains in the night.
Whose death is this? I will not see it.
What country's this? A world turned upside down.
I refuse the seeing.

The mourners go
From Willow Walk to Crofton Road,
By the Park to Farnborough Common.
Traffic jams. The Deputy Mayor
Of Margate, he'll be there to show respect.
A proper Romany funeral. Like an old queen's.
The ash tree, I say, the birch tree.
Such things need to be thought about before.
And the Devouring.
I refuse the seeing.

My death, I know it well:
The April day in nineteen thirty-three; the weather, rainy,
And cold; the missel-thrush singing all day
By the vardo, till I die. I am Urania,
Friend of the skies, the one who knows the future.

I will not hear the gypsies playing in the lager.
I will not hear it when the music stops.

13. AT STAUNTON HAROLD

> [He] founded this church
> Whose singular praise it is,
> to have done the best things in ye worst times,
> and
> hoped them in the most callamitous.

(over the west door at Staunton Harold church)

Many churches speak,
But this, in its despair, more eloquent than most.

The craftsmen who built it were looked after:
Shepheard artifex, the mason, who remembered
The tricks of the old trade; Smith the joiner;
Sam and Zachary, brothers, who created
Their own cloudy Creation overhead.

I'll see you safe, lads, he must have said,
No paperwork, no names, no packdrill.
I'll pay in cash. Money can't talk.

The church was unlawful, built doggedly
In the old proscribed fashion. But the founder's name
Runs clear as an indictment inside and out.
He didn't trouble to protect himself. Cromwell
Had him six times in the Tower, for weeks,
For months, suddenly for ever. He was twenty-seven,
And he died.

the best things

ye worst times

callamitous

hope.

NOTES

1. 'Found on the Battlefield': Bosworth Field, in Leicestershire, where Richard III was defeated by Henry VII in 1485. *The canal has invaded* ...: The Ashby Canal, created much later.

2. 'Lost and Lost'. *Under the great gold saltcellar* ...: This was described in a document as worth £66.12.4d. *Leicester City Centre*: Richard was ultimately buried in Grey Friars Church; this was destroyed at the Dissolution. The site is now covered by banks, shops and a car park.

3. 'The Master of the Cast Shadow': Portraits of this school show a combination of cast shadow and flat colour background. *The Master* was probably of German origin. *Barnet* (1471), *Towton* (1461), *Mortimer's Cross* (1461) were battles fought during the Wars of the Roses. *Red Gutters* ...: Such names are often given where battles have been fought.

4. 'Homily of the Hassocks': Sutton Cheney is a Leicester village on Richard's route from Leicester to Ambion Hill, where the Battle of Bosworth took place. Tradition says that St James's Church in Sutton Cheney was where Richard heard Mass for the last time, on 22 August.

5. 'Hats off, Gentlemen, a Genius': Pietro Torrigiano (1472–1522) was responsible for the monument of Henry VII in Westminster Abbey.

6. 'The Uses of Architecture': Victor Sage, 'Gothic Revival' in *The Handbook to Gothic Literature*, ed. M. Mulvey-Roberts (Macmillan, 1988).

7. 'Master Shakespeare: His Maggot'. *Burbage*: Richard Burbage, actor-manager.

8. 'Ask a Silly Question'. *Who's 'im* ...: old Punch joke.

9. 'Hundreds and Thousands': Brinklow, Warwickshire, is on the Oxford Canal.

10. 'Fox unearthed'. George Fox (1624–1691), the founder of Quakerism, was born at Drayton-in-the-Clay, Leicestershire (now Fenny Drayton), not far from the site of Richard's death at Bosworth Field. His youth coincided with the Civil War. Quotations and other material from George Fox's *Journal*.

11. 'The Fortune-Teller's Funeral': see *The Kentish Times*, 5.5.1933; Isabel Fonseca, *Bury Me Standing* (Vintage, 1996); Brian Vesey-FitzGerald, *Gypsies of Britain* (David & Charles, 1973). *The gypsy Z*: tattoo mark (for Zigeuner, meaning gypsy) used in Auschwitz-Birkenau. *Proper name*: Urania Boswell, wife of Levi. *Vardo*: Romany word for van. *Gorgio*: non-gypsy. *The Devouring*: gypsy word for the Holocaust.

12. 'At Staunton Harold'. Staunton Harold is in Leicestershire. The church was given to the National Trust in 1954; the Hall is leased to The Sue Ryder Foundation. Sir Robert Shirley (1629–1656) was the founder, and the unnamed hero of this section.

Née

She had strong views on Mrs Humphry Ward,
The Brontës, poor souls, women called George,
Novelists known as A Lady.

There was always
An edginess. Whenever we went too far,
Children or parent, she'd flare *O you Fanthorpes!*
As if at some foreign breed.

She lost some magic when she married us.
Not race or class, but a sense of being her.
Red hair was part of it, and the surname
That gave her the convent's nickname, *Reddy*.

Marriage turned her *Ginger*, and unsettled her.
We knew the men who might have been our father,
Doctor, diplomat, soldier. We understood
They'd have had better, smarter children.

The way she said *My* family left us standing.
Racier than anything we knew, her father,
The seventh son, who wouldn't marry the heiress,
Walked from Devon to London, his flute in his pocket;

Her handsome mother, lover of dogs, not children,
Descendant of the gentle Tudor scholar,
Who never used a fullstop in her life.

She did everything well. Had a head for figures,
Understood the Married Women's Property Act.
Created faultless parcels, Fs and Ps flamboyant,
Converted the exile of marriage into art.

Vaguely we knew we'd missed something by happening.
We were the children of Mrs Humphry Ward.
Marriage is burial, she used to say.

I could have written novels, or played the french horn.

Kinch & Lack

(Boys' Outfitters)

Elderly man with a tape-measure.
Pedantic; a shade arch
(I don't see this at the time),
Treats my brother like a bride.

My mother not at ease
(I feel, but don't know why);
My brother, flattered, diffident,
Somehow aware of destiny.

Youngest son faces his kingdom
And his trousseau, socks, cap, scarf,
Wreathed in official colours
For unimagined deeds,

Greek, rugger, chemistry, things
He will do and I shan't,
Though I am two years older,
Taller, have read more books.

He's rehearsed for a special future
By a man with pins in his mouth;
Seven-year Dante, whose Vergil
Salutes his inches with respectful craft.

Mother stands restlessly by,
The cheque-book in her bag
(And I know, without being told,
There's a world enlisting him
That hasn't a place for me.

O.K. I'll make my own).

Mother Scrubbing the Floor

She had a dancer's feet, elegant, witty.
We had our father's, maverick spreaders of dirt.

Dirt from London, dirt from Kent,
Mud, dust, grass, droppings, wetness, things,
Dirt barefaced, dirt stinking, dirt invisible.

Whatever it was, she was ready:
The rubber kneeler, clanking galvanised bucket,
The Lifebuoy, the hard hot water.

Let me! we'd say, meaning *Hate to see you do this.*
Too old. Too resentful. Besides, you'll blame us
That you had to do it.

She never yielded. We couldn't do it right,
Lacking her hatred of filth, her fine strong hands.

Don't want you to do this, she said. *Don't want you to have to.*
Just remember this: love isn't sex
But the dreary things you do for the people you love.
Home is the girl's prison
The woman's workhouse, she said.
Not me, she said. *Shaw.*

I do remember. I stand where she knelt.

Against Speech

Harpo's the wittiest Marx. Words are only
For what can be said; silence
Has a better vocabulary.

Disposable the expensive eloquence
Of QCs, DJs, MPs,
Hairdressers, headmasters, hot gospellers, humorists,
Ball-by-ball cricket commentators, consultants,
Voice recognition software from IBM.

O for a tongue-tied muse to celebrate
The steadfast dumbness of dissidents under torture,
The hangdog faces of children who won't perform,
Quakers, clever as fish in a soundless dimension,
Lovers in crowded trains.

But something must be said for the unemphatic
Chat of World Service at four o'clock in the morning,
Of nurses checking at midnight in drowsy wards,
Of parents talking things over together downstairs
When everyone else is in bed. These are
The great protectors; their half-heard patter
Signals *All's well; all's well; so far, all's well.*

Words for Months

Their names in this country
Wore out, though the weather
Is still what they charted:

After-Yule; Mud-month; Mad
(The one that wants to knock
You down and plant a tree

On top of you); Easter
(Her month, the spring lady);
Three-milkings-a-day month

(Everyone smelling of
Cow); First-nice-month; Second-
Nice month (our fathers had no

Word for spade but spade); Weed;
Holy; Leaf-fall; Shambles
(Cattle-culling month); and

Here-we-are-again Yule.

Someone has overlaid
This tired chronicle
Of endless days, thin lives

With shoddy Roman goods –
War, doorways, emperors,
Even the numbers wrong.

They fit better, the dull
Words for difficult things:
Mud. Milk. Weeds. Leaf-fall. Cull.

(Se aeftera Geola; Sol-monath; Hreth-monath; Easter-monath; Thrimylce;
Se aerra Litha; Se aeftera Litha; Weod-monath: Halig-monath; Winter-fylleth;
Blot-monath; Se aerra Geola. (from W. W. Skeat, *A Student's Pastime*, 1896).)

Strong Language in South Gloucestershire

Vocabulary of earth, names

Tough and diehard as crypts,
Cathedrals perched on their shoulders.

No committee okayed them.
They happened, like grass,

Written down all anyhow
By cosmopolitan clerks in a hurry.

Ramshackle riddles, their meaning
Deconstructed in aloof universities,

Their proper stresses a password
Known only to cautious locals.

Now, inscribed on steel, they confront drivers,
Looming on roads by the restriction signs,

Unreel their quirks along the prim
Mensuration of Ordnance Survey,

Still hard at it, still proclaiming
Here are Soppa's tinpot two acres,

Something holy, a good place for blackbirds,
Duck farm, bridge over mud,

The strangers' bright city.

(Various Sodburys; Nympsfield; Ozleworth; Doughton; Slimbridge; Gloucester. These are all places in Gloucestershire.)

Three Poems for Amy Cook (1909–1998)

1. AMY SITS FOR HER PORTRAIT

(for Peter and Victoria)

Like a pre-Cambrian hill, she looks down
Mildly at our callow landscape.
We stare, we ask. She endures, having learned
Over years to perform herself.

Her part is *racy rustic*, which she isn't.
Her standards are her own, so clearly better
She never explains them. We have to guess
Why she's brought her private shepherd's pie,

Solid among the pâtés and lasagne; why,
As we slop about in the sun, in shorts and sneakers,
She's upright in straw hat and floral print;
Why she takes posing seriously; why she sings,

Recites, talks about education; why the dogs
Revere her, lying in the shade behind her chair;
Why she never tells her age; why she's always saying
Rome wasn't built in a day. So old,

So many dead-end jobs, so clever, now
She lives in a different country, translates
Patiently into our language, knows how to tell her life
As if it were a story. She has the poise

Of one who never had a chance,
And yet is always listened to.
Not a *turn*, though that's how she plays it.

The speechless portrait speaks the truth.
Don't listen. Look.

2.   AMY TELLS US

Why she brings her private shepherd's pie:

I d'like bacon. Don't like brown bread.
The chips was lovely. Piece of fish
I ad were cremated. I gave they
To the fowls.

Why she takes posing seriously:

I only ave to sit yur and
See the scenery. Whatever you want,
Love, don't be afraid to move it.
You can fiddle as much as you like.
There's sittens, and there's fidgets.
If e ain't right, say so.

Why she sings:

I d'know a few ditties.
Some o they modern songs be all right.

and recites:

'Behold, a giant am I!
Aloft here in my tower ...'
(Moving her arms as they taught her at school.
Gets to the end, without flaw.)

and talks about education:

At school, they did teach we to remember.
When I did learn the alphabet, I did learn it
Frontards and backards. (And does it.)
Teachers wasn't afraid of kids in they days.
I did like Grimms' Tales. I know

Tis only imagination, but I did like en.
They did turn out good scholars in they days.

She won't tell her age. But she will tell you

I wasn't built in a day.

3.   A TOUCH OF ECLAIR

A golden day for our dog when, passing that Coombe cottage,
She was given a chocolate eclair. Ever after,
Our dog appalled Long Street drivers, bounding over to Amy.

Old and straight like Westridge beeches,
We see her now in paintings, not as she was,
Waiting outside the Co-op with her shopping.

Swift and surprising, like the road from Nibley,
Her wit and her way with words. Gloucester
Has an archive; they study her vowels in Birmingham.

The endless bone-weary work she did on roads round Wotton
To clean them for us. Fish and chip paper,
Toffee papers, sweet papers, *all the ruddy lot.*

Something grand, something gold about Amy. Thin, old, poor,
She blessed us all with her blunt presence. A touch of eclair
At her funeral, when the Silver Band played her out.

For SO 759934: 14.2.96. A Love-poem

She is my Corinna, my Lucasta,
Whose name, for courtesy, I will not say.

Like a tomboy, she sprawls among sharp small hills;
Like a sibyl, she drifts into silences and fog.

She has her own way with birds and flowers;
Is given to minor fierce festivals without much notice.

Her speech is like a mouthful of hot chestnuts.
Extra hs and ls give her vowels grace.

Her lovely highborn sisters over the hill
With their suitors and reputations look down on her.

She doesn't care, preferring her laidback cronies,
Symn, Bradley, Haw, Bear, Ragnall and Shinbone.

Her favourite scent: a dab of woodsmoke behind the ears.
Haute couture and haute cuisine are not her style.

She is an early riser, watery and echoing;
I love her then. And in the evening, when blackbirds call it a day.

In all the seasons of every year I love her.
And this seems as good a day as any to say so.

Conygre Wood and Hyakinthoides Non-Scriptus

(for Libby Houston)

This is how it is, here:
Native halflight. Rain off the Atlantic.
Rack of blue like sky growing
A foot above ground. Hush. Birdcalls.
Small puckered beech leaves, and earth,
Its muscles showing, hurdling up limestone,
With acres of blue on its back.

Disappointment to the early masters,
Dons, doctors, name-givers,
Like getting a girl when you wanted a boy.
They hoped for Hyakinthos, the beautiful,
Whose literate petals say *AI AI*
Sorry Sorry, inscribed by divine Apollo,
Who killed the lovely creature by mistake.

But our island gets this lot, illiterate
Non-scriptus flowers. Growing along with garlic,
Smelling of honey, careless of Latin snubs.
Blue and blue and blue and free
Of an invented grief, free
To come and go, to multiply, to chant
The noiseless bluebell anthem: *Here we are.*

The Offshore Trip

It's not far really.
The by-laws will be the same,
And the flora. Language will be banal
In familiar ways. And yet
This small elementary act of crossing the water
Implies another chance, a different world.

(We crossed in an open boat.)

Safety announcements about dressing warmly,
Remaining calm in an emergency.
How far are we going? What shipwrecks underlie
This modest channel?

(It was a still November evening.)

Gulls cry prosaically. The galley
Smells of bacon. Look! we are never
Out of sight of land. Two ferries
Edge past each other in the seaway
Like ceremonious topheavy tea-cosies.

(One dark heron flew over the Solent
Backed by a daffodil sky.)

We have artless designs. Mr Tennyson
Is looking for a house; a holiday, a visit –
That's about it. But inscrutable dark doings
Fidget us somewhere. Without knowing how we know,
We know of the dead great king, the open boat
Stuffed with gold and swords, ice on the thwarts,

Give way, and the people wailing,
Their luck-bringer gone. They let the sea take him,
Not knowing where that cargo would fetch up.

This we know and don't know as we board the ferry.

[The parentheses indicate quotations from the diary of Emily Tennyson. The dead king is Scyld, king of the Danes, whose ship-burial is described at the beginning of *Beowulf*.]

The Burren

Undomesticated. A great grey
Migrainous cramp of rock,
Squeezed, compressed and scoured
To treeless dryness, and in the air,
The noise of waters underground.

Bloody-minded sort of place, it looks,
Where old faiths shrivel, old names are defaced.
But out of these barren flags, this crazed landscape,
Jut the resilient heads of a melting-pot
Of flowers from the high and cold, the low and hot,
The wet, wet places. All at ease on this rockface.

Like finding love in someone disliked at first.

And the boy out shooting rabbits put his fingers
In a rocky crack, touched the smoothness
Of a king's gold breastplate left behind
At Gleninsheen. These flybynight findings
Wait within gunshot in unpromising places –
Gold breastplates, gentians, happiness-ever-after.

Seven Types of Shadow

1.

I have an item, Chair, under Any Other Business.
We ghosts have become creatures of habit, with our
Bloody shrouds, bloody footprints, blood. Some of us,
I believe, still hold our heads under our arms.

The agenda is stale, gentleghosts. Midnight. The temperature drops.
Dogs' hackles rise. Tawny owls provide
The continuo. A chain rattles. A floorboard creaks.
We know the repertoire. *So do the living.*

You see how it is, fellow-ghosts. We are fossilised.
Something unconventional's needed; the ghost, perhaps,
Of a happy moment. Try this: wraith of a spectral grandee,
Whose horse has just won the Derby. A lady might like that.

He throws his topper in the air, a champagne shade.
Or a musical ghost, ghost of divine Handel,
Scribbling down the final *Hallelujah,*
Thinking he's just seen heaven. How about that?

2.

Furthermore, ghosts, the matter of dialogue.
A surplus of vowels is ours – all those *ooos* and *aaas.*
Think of the vital things we could be saying,
Like *I've finished the Pope's ceiling! All of it!*

Or *One hundred and fifty-four sonnets! Not bad, Ben?*
Or, in the mist and snow, *I fancy this might be the top,*
Or *I tried it on the dairymaid, and it worked.*
Or – surprisingly – *We are a grandmother!*

3.

This is a country of ghosts. Down the eastern shore
Lie the drowned villages, drowned luggers, drowned sailors.

After a hot summer, fields grow talkative.
Wheat speaks in crop marks, grasses in parch marks.

Wheat or grass, what they tell is the truth
Of things that lay underneath five thousand years ago,

The forts, the barrows, the barns, the shrines, the walls.
These are the native ghosts. After a hot summer.

No haunting. No rattle of chains. They just lie there
In their rigid truthfulness, the ghosts of things.

4.

We carry our human ghosts around with us.
As we grow we face the mirrors, and see

The spectre of a great-aunt, a vague look
Known only from sepia snapshots. The hands we're used to –

Yes, these – their contours came by way of a long retinue
Of dust. We are photofits of the past,

And the future eyes us sideways as we eye ourselves.
We are the ghosts of great-aunts and grand-nephews.

We are ghosts of what is dead and not yet born.

5.

And here's a man as near a ghost
As you can be, and not be dead.
He haunts his world from love,
Before his world's awake.

His personal early morning. He moves with it,
Shredding the nightshift behind. World Service
Croons *Lillibullero* in his ear, and confides
What no one yet knows: a statesman disgraced;
Bomb in the Paris Metro; goal after extra time
In Argentina. He notes the emergency windows, bright and busy
With midwives, students, bankrupts, lovers, thieves.

These are the pinched hours, scrounged from blackout,
Too soon for milk or mail. Even the cocks
Not alerted yet. Engine silenced, he coasts
The inhabited yards to home, shuts and opens and shuts
As if doors were silk. The sleepers sprawl
In their private zigzags. He walks *sotto voce*,
As if they were all sick children. *Lillibullero*.

He has perverse cravings, to mow the lawn, to sing,
Or hoover, or run a bath. Smell's risky as sound.
No bacon. Not even the modest tang of toast.
Conscious of power, knowing he could shatter
The tenuous fringes of sleep, like a small
Insignificant god, he bestows on them quiet, peace,
The useful dreams that come at the edge of morning.

Passive, he waits for the world to move his way,
To want to know who won after extra time
In Argentina. *Lillibullero*.

6.
Ghosts of past, present, future.
But the ones the living would like to meet are the echoes
Of moments of small dead joys still quick in the streets,

Voices calling *I've passed* / *We won* / *QED* /
It didn't hurt much, Mum / *They've given me the job* /
I have decided to name this apple Bramley;

And the women convicts singing their Holloway march,
While Ethel Smyth conducts from her cell with a toothbrush.

7.

These are the ghosts the living would prefer,
Ghosts who'd improve our ratings. Ghosts
Of the great innocent songs of freedom
That shoulder their way round the world like humpback whales,

Ghosts of the singers, the dancers, the liberated,
Holding hands and cheering in parks, while the tanks
Squat immobilised. Ghosts of the women on the fish quay
Hugging each other when at last the boats come in.

Ghosts of the last night of the Proms. And ghosts of lovers,
Wandering round London, so happy that they could
Have danced danced danced all night.

New Highgate Cemetery: 4 April 1996

(i.m. Tom Wakefield)

Passover. And the rabbi's taking a risk
(Somebody hints) to be at a gentile funeral
On the holiest day.* After the general amens,
In a low voice, moved, he speaks the prayer for the dead.

Maundy Thursday. The glamorous vicar, stripped
To a showy scarlet cassock, circulates
After the burial. Embraces shoulders,
Rubs his face against other wet faces. Borrows a hanky.

From Tottenham to Arsenal, Chelsea to Crystal Palace,
Florists have been picked clean. All flowers are here,
Banked up, as if honouring murdered babies,
Taking their chance of the April frosts with Tom.

Aintree week. So Tom should have been laying
His arcane bets. But death, the rank outsider,
Chose a different winning-post, and here,
In a recklessness of flowers, Tom lies, the right

Place at last, among comrades, campaigners, jokers,
Near the surly shadow of Marx. His heart gave out,
As we might have expected, used too much
For loving whoever, whatever would let him love.

We have lost his teacher's searchlight eye, that located
Not back-row trouble, but goodness all over; his novelist's ear,
That listened to the vague, the stumbling,
And knew what they meant; we have lost

His running-to-meet-you heart, that ignored
The tactics of learning and power, but cared so much
About being simply human. This over-the-top
Stuff would embarrass him. Stop. Say *Sorry, Tom.*

---

* In fact, the Sabbath is the 'holiest day' for Jews while Passover is regarded as a
Jewish festival.

Underground

(Henry Moore's *A Shelter Sketchbook*)

They have come as far as there is,
Under the tree-roots, the sewers,
Under drains, cables, flood-plains.

They sprawl, wrapped in blankets,
Waiting like tubers for spring, the all-clear.
At Belsize Park, Cricklewood,

The Liverpool Street Extension,
Londoners lie under London, incubating
A difficult energy, a different life.

Round the corner the artist watches,
Jotting notes on an envelope.
To have drawn from life would be like

Sketching in the hold of a slave ship.
Not the Cockney wags of legend, but huge
Muffled forms, trussed and bandaged

Like Lazarus. Wood and stone,
As well as bones and veins, wait inside
These vast vulnerabilities.

From their coding, we can construe
Houses falling, bridges falling, London falling,
Civilisations falling down. The artist

Must show this without saying. Just
His sketchbook's sotto-voce: *Abstractish figures shelter background,*
And *Try white again then scramble dryish grey over.*

Also he shows the women knitting,
People holding hands, sleeping,
And thinking. Particularly thinking.

From these rhizomes the future will rise,
Equivocal, chancy. Crowned stones
On a northern moor, too big for houses,

And paper-shrouded Cardboard Citizens,
Sleeping in Strand doorways, neighbours to rubbish,
And all stations between. As Cabot

Aimed for Japan, got Newfoundland instead,
These monstrous eggs may hatch surprisingly.

Above them, paving stones and tarmac sag,
Windows taped into resistance, the hunched
Apprehensive roofs of Cricklewood

And Belsize Park, the Liverpool Street Extension,
Guns, smoke, cloud, fighters, bombers, fire, air,

Under the City, in the sky, pitched
Between heaven and humanity, as we are,
The tube trains shuttling between,

And the artist taking notes round the corner.

Torched, they might have been, in another country
Because the wrong people lived in them;
Or, in quieter times, in homelier places,
Left to slither modestly back to earth.

But this is London. There are guide-lines.
Houses are groomed for a protracted ending.

Some house-man has been on his rounds, diagnosing
The slow-motion stages of a terminal event.
Amputate, he prescribed. First went the more portable shrubs,
The carpets, fittings. Lastly, the people.

Then experts came. They blinded each window
With hardboard, extracted knockers and bells like teeth;
As nurses raise screens in wards to island the dying,
They erected eight-foot boards to segregate.

(And someone has aerosoled *Save us* and *Help*,
Help and *Save us*, along the new wood.)

An avenue-full of confident thirties semis,
Twin-gabled, porched, with double mock-Tudor chimneys,
Who shopped at the Army and Navy, golfed in Ealing,
Dentists, dog-walkers, Dry Fly drinkers – that sort of house.

Now they tremble together, W12 Samsons;
Rooftops flayed of tiles are all you can see.
Tomorrow men in heavy duty yellow jackets
With JCBs will rubbish the garlanded plaster.

(And the forsythia gamely still in flower,
And the houses opposite watching speechless
Like aristos brought too soon in their tumbrils,
Watching the load before them.)

This was the way the world marched on.
This may be how it starts. *Atrocity*
Is what we haven't got used to yet.

Maud Speaking

When I came to the gate alone
  You were making eyes at a lily,
Conversing in such an intimate tone
  That I felt remarkably silly.
Your grotesque behaviour I cannot condone.
  Your welcome I found chilly.

A poet, I know, may be queer.
  One learns to be dignified.
One would rather not interfere.
  One has one's feminine pride.
That very long poem about Mr Arthur Henry Hallam
  One took in one's stride.

But a man who talks all night
  To a larkspur and a rose –
Is something wrong with your sight?
  I thought you meant to propose,
But when I arrived you ignored me quite.
  I might as well have been prose.

And I didn't care for the stuff
  You wrote about my head;
Little head, like a light-minded bit of fluff;
  But I'm tolerably well read,
Would have studied at Newnham, under Miss Clough,
  If Papa hadn't sworn *better dead*.

Away, melancholy!
  Lord Tennyson, goodbye.
I'm up to here with botany,
  I want someone streetwise and spry.
There are plenty of suitable fish in the sea.
  Poets need not apply.

Gospel Truth

(for Matt Simpson)

I am the one who sees,
    Whose eyes out-eye the sun.
Who flies beyond the mind
    Who knows all that is done.
All words, all theories
    For me spell out the One.
I am the eye that sees;
    I am the eagle, John.

I am the one who tells
    The dreadful descent of man:
Adam, Attila, Gandhi,
    Hero and hooligan.
We all inherit beastliness
    Some of us light on grace;
I am Mark, the archivist,
    Mark with the lion's face.

I learned my art in hospitals
    Where life begins and ends;
Where some refuse and some consent
    And nobody much attends.
And some are called to be sacrificed,
    The lobster, the lamb, the fox;
I honour the One who consents to death,
    Luke stands for the ox.

This is the one who walks,
    Who knows the people's names,
The shops, the cinemas, the docks,
    The pubs, the children's games;
Who loves the living and the dead
    Of the place where he began,
The holy city, Liverpool.
    Matthew celebrates man.

This and That: Guido Morris at St Ives

Once every cottage housed its potter or painter
(Sculpture took up more space), and they kept on the move,
Chasing a better north light, more tolerant neighbours.

They used ephemera to chart their lives:
Change of phone number, price-list, wife.
Small things some need to know, others to hear.

Familiar unexciting scraps of this and that.

Here to these on-off quarters by the sea
Came Guido, Master of the Latin Press
                    which
HAS BEEN ESTABLISHED TO THE GLORY OF GOD
                    AND
        OF THE ARTS OF PEACE
                    offering

        MOTOR and BODY REPAIRS
        J and J COUCH LIMITED
                    or
        Tickets price 4s, 3s 6p,
                2s and 1s
        may be had from the
        Business Manager.

He treasured the things he worked with, the Bembo fount,
Hard-biting old presses, and paper, the heart of the job,
The hand-made paper of England.
You can gauge the love by the work he did:
By the long-tailed capital   R s.
By his feeling for names like Jack B. Yeats –
            Jack
            B
            Yeats.

54

He was impractical. Ran out of full-stops.
Charged too much, or too little. Didn't finish.
Lost touch with helpful friends. And drank; and drank.

The painters and potters lost their singular printer.
The Underground took him. Gill Sans-serif ogled him,
From Barking to Bond Street, Richmond to Rotherhithe.

How the trains lunge, hesitate, shake and stall,
And the faces focus and fade, and are never known.
He served for twenty years, having no choice.

Unique Guido, who cherished the twenty-six
Soldiers of lead which can conquer the world,
Who did the right thing but never got it right;

Who chose narrow paper, and narrowed words to fit,
Like CATALO
        GUE; who used your civilised craft
On Wine Lists, Baptist Teas, notes about ration books.

From the long future, greeting. Be well.

      FLOREANT
      ARTES HU
      MANITATIS

Overheard at Lumb Bank

(two tutors consult)

E D:

Let's toss for it. Shall it be you
Or shall it be me that speaks
To Emily about her punctuation?

W W:

There's been a complaint from Heptonstall
About Bill. He's asking kids questions.
Not exactly *accosting*, no. But odd things, like
How many in family? Are they stepping westward?
Might lead to something. You can't be too careful.
You'd better watch it, Bill, I said to him.
I'd rather you stuck to daffodils while you're here.

The Visitor:

The tall one? She isn't on my list. Seems
To have just walked in. Don't know
About her stuff. It seems
Familiar, somehow. *Rialto*, would you say,
Or *Outposts*? I get the impression
She might be local.

A T:

Well, I can see you've worked really hard at this.
All these rough drafts you've kindly brought along.
I respect your dedication. But I don't know
If anybody's going to publish it.

Friendship. Bit of a coy word, wouldn't you say
In this day and age? Come clean about *in* or *out*,
Alfred, then we'll know who your readers are.
And while we're at it, all these Greeks or whatever
– Gods, sorry – really, they won't do.
This one. Tithonus? Never heard of her.
How d'you pronounce it? How many readers know that?
And this rhyme scheme of yours, *abba*,
It really does go on, you know. Monotonous.
Depressing, too. Sorry to be so tough,
But you've come here for help; that's what you're getting.

Petition of the Cats concerning Mr Peter Porter

This from the congregation of the cats:
Our candidate is house-trained; endures
Fur on his trousers, fishbreath up his nose,
Sick on the carpet, dead mice in dark places.

Though of a migratory nature, he's exact
About returning home to your deponents.
Here he communes with gods called Bark and Persil,
Speaks on paper, air and the electrics

Of things unknown to cats, but in tones we trust.
He reads in books, is globally learned.
Your excellencies know of course that Mr P
Is a major poet. Cats, though they dance, sing and skylark,

Have not mastered this craft, but we understand
Certain of our tribe have been celebrated in it,
Namely one Jeoffry, several Practicals, and a small
One singing on a train. Mr Porter speaks well of cats,

And all small harried things. He minds
About myxomatosis; spit-roasting chickens
Spit *Auschwitz*, to him; he sees *the unbending
Seriousness of small creatures.*

Remember this, excellencies: the learning,
Pity, wisdom (considering too the recent incumbent's
Taste for beaks, claws, hooks, teeth and other ungentle things),
We present our candidate as Poet Laureate (Creatures).

Thank you for your attention.

Postcards

(for Christine Wells)

The walkabout postman studies his handful
Before he slots them home. What do they say?

Public as T-shirts, coded like
A mole's correspondence, designed to be enigmatic.

Having a wonderful they say. *Oh boy,*
This is the life! or *Cooler now. Had to put*

Our cardies on, they say, or *Natives friendly,*
Or just *Wish you were here.* He knows, the postman,

They don't say what they mean, mean what they say.
Extraordinary too, he thinks, the cards they send:

Of opera houses: owls; folk being ethnic;
Fish; teapots; *eucryphia milleganii*

(What'll she make of that? he thinks, popping it in.)
Each picture sends a message – proud, witty, wise –

But not enough for him to understand.
(*Super day yesterday sorry I missed the post.*)

O postman, postman, endlessly chivvied by cliché,
This freakish correspondence that teases you so
Is a minor rehearsal for the final take-off.

Look in the graveyard, as you make your round;
There are the ultimate postcards, trite as ever,
Stylised as runes, with a subtext intricate

As a crossword puzzle clue, or house-agent's blurb,
Delivering the last message of stay-at-homes
To those who have left on a journey beyond deliveries:

Gone, not forgotten; Sadly missed; Wish you were here.

Look, No Hands

(*Lala at the Fernando Circus*, by Edgar Degas. National Gallery, London)

He:
It was hard doing this. I had to go up near the roof,
Among the girders and dusty bits. And I had to keep
On trying till I found the right place to be –
Left, and in front; not very far below her
So I could make you see how hard it is.

You have to imagine the audience. I didn't
Bother with them, they're always the same,
Ooh-ing, aah-ing, clapping, some of them
Shutting their eyes. And the smells. You have
To imagine them too: people, horses, sawdust, sweat.

You're lucky. I'm showing you what the audience
Can't really see. Far off, up in the roof,
Something between a bird and an angel, using
Arms like wings. Hovering, you could say;
Not holding on. See how she does it?

Neither a bird nor an angel, she flies
With a metal bar in her teeth. And that strong mouth
Hauls her up, up, up, in her white and gold,
So that it all looks easy. So that she flies.

She:
All right, I suppose. Doesn't look much like me,
But it's me all right, my act. He's better
Than the usual gawpers. *How much d'you weigh?* they say,
Or *Are your teeth your own?* He painted my boots O.K.
I told him they cost a bomb.

The Witness

Picturesque as Raskolnikov,
The accused in the dock,
Probing the metaphysic of offence.

Apprentice, uncomfortable, the jury
Cranes towards every opening mouth,
Knowing that sooner or later there will be a verdict,
And they will be guilty of it.

Solicitors, counsel, clerk, have a place,
And are easy there. At home, they remember,
A separate life of hugging, smoking,
Solving the crossword, asking what's for dinner.

The judge sits above, like a tennis umpire;
Now and then he mentions the rules of the game.
He is accustomed to scarlet, horsehair, ermine.
Intimidation is not his intention,
But what he achieves. Let us now

Examine the witness. He is the outsider,
He belongs to another court, pursuing
A different code. He is messenger
Of what happened, expert without diploma,
Suspect as a prisoner, innocent as a judge.

All he can say is what he saw,
And that's an old story. Cross-examined,
He flounders. His vigilance is fishy,
His ignorance shady. Truth is hard to translate
When our only machinery is words.

Popular Fallacies

that snow is somehow holy; that bleak midwinters
are commonplace events in Palestine;

that snow is snow-white (wrong. It's eyelid colour,
colour of blood at the farthest end of the wound);

that it blesses (it doesn't; its spiteful tally of wrens,
explorers, old people sitting in chairs,

kingfishers, match-girls, gives it away). Affable thug, that
has it in for the poor, small, brave, bluffing

the rest of us with your rubber-stamping sameness; snuffer-
out of difference, hypocrite white-out,

landhungry dictator with your whiteshirts, your overnight putsch,
your doubletalk about absolution,

watch it! under your white sepulchre the fifth column of
the future is waiting, new, particular,

bright green.

Sightings

1.
It was there all the time, the dark planet
That no one saw. Mathematicians nagged,
Convinced it was there by the frolic
Detours of the others. Such heavenly high jinks
Offended their neat minds. A flurry
Of sums across Europe, and lo! Neptune
Exists (official). Fireworks. National pride. Letters
In learned journals. Unmoved, the great
Green gassy planet perseveringly
Coasts its majestic journey through the dark.

2.
The town's there all the time, under the mist.
Well, of course it is. I walked up from it,
Alone with the dog, the early birds
And a sun so private all it could achieve
Was a bar of light on hawthorn
And the crocketed tips of the church tower
Springing up from the meadow of fog below
Chanting *Glory glory* in thin gold voices.
Beneath the haze a town's work is hatching,
Quick, bright, smelling of herbs and bread.

3.
There's two of each of us, I think he thinks,
But indistinguishable. There's one from Ephesus
And one from Syracuse. The audience knows,
But we don't. That's the point; the strangeness
Of the other who is the same.
Twins pop up everywhere. King Claudius, King Hamlet,
Goneril and Regan, Falstaff and the King,
Hoping to be part of the last act magic
Moment of revelation, when yes, there are two,
But also one, joined by something darker than love.

Afterwards

The principalities, the powers, the politicians,
The ones who pose in the spotlight
Centre-stage, and magnetise us as they stalk
Towards bankruptcy, murder, betrayal, suicide,
And other traditional exits

The audience leaves, discussing nuances.
A scatter of sweet-papers, ash,
Smells hanging around behind. The audience leaves.

And in they come, rolling up their sleeves,
With hoovers and mops, buckets and brushes and Brasso,
Making it ready for the next time, nobody watching,
With small uncompetitive jokes, with backchat
About coach-trips, soaps, old men,
And a great sloshing of water.

This is where we ought to be. Not
Up on the stage with the rich and the Richards,
Rehearsing already their entry for the next house,
The precise strut that registers power,

But down on our hands and knees,
Laughing, and mopping up.

Another Swan Poem

This swan knows too much poetry.
It came knocking at the window

Importunate, drumming Tap-Tap
Like a midnight lover. This is

Early morning for us, Swan. It
Takes not a blind bit of. It stands

On water, wings spreadeadling,
Neck rampant, mouthing *Me. You. Now.*

Eat. Now. You. Me. No magic shirt,
No ducal coronet, just bare

Swan, mouthing *Me. Eat. You.* Nervous,
We fetch the brown sliced. The snake-neck

Lunges as we cast Hovis on
The water. Vindictively it

Dunks, drowns, swallows. Rears up again.
Romance is what it wants. Savage

Black eyes peer close. We can number
The brownish forehead feathers. Far

Too near. The long beak opens, long
And oval-ended, containing

A sharp active tongue. The creature
Seeks to be seductive. Wants us

To slot our bread inside its beak.
We do it, gingerly, trying

Not to touch. It accepts the slice,
Dips it, comes back, until the last

Scatter of crumbs. Reluctantly
It navigates away. A faint

Me. You. comes sighing down the water.

This is not a good poem about a swan,
But it might be the bravest. It is also true.

Olive

Generosity: the gift of the gods. This one
Is famous for giving Athens a singular tree.

We met in my office door. She'd jammed
Her hoover in it. *Sorry, my lover,* she said.

Don't like to leave it in the passage.
Patients fall over things. Daily thereafter

She'd hail me: *Still yur, then?* And once,
Thassa funny name you got. Latin, ennit? I'm Olive.

Now you know. Her first gift, drink. A cup of tea (hot)
By my phone every day when I came to work.

Thought you could do with it. All that way
Yew as to come. No kettle, ave yer?

Thought not. Not like they nurses,
Always at the Tetleys. Next came food

(A Welsh cake) on Fridays. *Nice recipe, ennit?*
Our Nan's. From the Forest, she wuz. After that, learning

(She was famous for it). *Bit ignorant about Bristol,*
Aren't yer? Ave a read of me book.

Later, understanding. *Yer won't learn much about patients*
From doctors and nurses. Yew as to get to like em.

We're in there ages doing them toilets. It all adds up.

She decided I needed laugher. Every day
Was waiting in my office with a joke,

Selected specially, just right for me –
Not rude or stale or obvious. Not easy, either.

She watched me like a suspect. Had I got there?
Or was my laugh just half a bar too late?

Her final gift was cryptic. She put
Three flaky bulbs in my hand when I left,

And *See what comes of they*, she said.
What came was lilies. Came, and keep on coming,

Tall and immortal in a mortal garden.

Athene, the wise goddess, presented Athens with the olive tree, the gift most useful
to mortals.

Post-op.

Artists are wrong about light. They strew it
Tastefully across landscapes, let it focus
Thoughtfully on a forehead or a cabbage,
Self-consciously walk down a reach of water.

Artists are wrong.

Light comes storming out of its corner
Dealing dazzling uppercuts to the eyes.

See, says Light, *It's like this and like this*,
Injecting the whole national grid into one lens;

This is what you were missing, says Light,
Grinning like a mouthful of American teeth;

Fizzing and raucous, like the mixture
In Dr Jekyll's retort; importunate, like the tune

A child has just acquired for one finger.
That's good, says Light, *I knew you'd like it*,

And demonstrates
The unexpected awfulness of the tiles on the kitchen floor.

Q's Pew (Fowey Church)

'I had rather be a doorkeeper ...' Psalm 84, v. ii.

Up at God's end, the grandees: Treffrys and Rashleighs,
In layers of granite, epitaph and swagger.

We looked for him there. It seemed the right place
For a knight, a mayor, a writer, a Cambridge professor,

Begetter of English studies. Up there with the choir;
Or, rather less classy, near the Spanish galleon's

Fancy woodwork converted to Protestant pulpit.
He must have relished that. But not there, either.

He lurks in a lowly place, in a one-bum pew,
An edging of seat, left over from a pillar.

His wife perched here with him. He'd sit at the outer end
In his courtly way. A small brass plaque

Tells us nothing much (which is all there's room for),
Leaving us free to guess. I like him for being modest,

For sitting so far from the haves, in the draught
Near the south door. Not quite a doorkeeper. He'd be too old.

But nearness to doorkeepers may have seemed better
Than nearness to grandees and God for a man like him.

Autumn Offer

Vacancies available now
For the next millennium's consumers, investors,
And personnel. We supply
State-of-the-art instruction – the leaner, fitter curriculum
Your youngster needs. Already
We have axed from our course the modules that clearly
Have long passed their sell-by-date:
Art, music, history, literature, religion.
Currently we are phasing out language,
But retaining Japanese and German,
For obvious reasons.

(Season of timetables, and uniform ...)

Up-to-the-minute hard/software is
Our speciality, thanks to the funding of
Our sponsors, whose logo you will notice. In view of
Such high-tech resources, we're talking
Economies of scale staff-wise. We're sure
Parents will appreciate the forward nature of this move.

(Season of texts, and learning what to think ...)

Due to our expertise in counselling we guarantee
To painlessly re-program, and remove
All juvenile addictions: drugs,
Cloudsofglory, sex, humour,
Imagination, cheating, hope,
Etc. Research tells us these
No longer enjoy street cred.

(Season of learning to be like the rest ...)

Our youngsters must learn to grow up
Aggressive, acquisitive, mean. We put them in teams

And train them to slog it out
According to the rules (union, league,
Whatever). Most of life's problems can be solved
By running fast and kicking something.

Four Christmas Carols

1. THE GARDENER AT CHRISTMAS

He has done all that needs to be done.

Rake, fork, spade, cleaned and oiled,
Idle indoors; seeds, knotty with destiny, rattle
Inside their paper jackets. The travelling birds
Have left; predictable locals
Mooch in the early dusk.

He dreams of a future in apples,
Of three white lilies in flower,
Of a tree that could bear a man.

He sits back and waits
For it all to happen.

2. CHRISTMAS TRAFFIC

Three, two, one, zero. liftoff
Signals Mission Control. And off they go
To the dark parts of the planets
In their pressurised spacesuits,
Cocooned in technology, the astronauts.

Mission control whispers in someone's ear.
Yes, she says, *I will.* And in due time
A different traveller makes a quieter journey,
Arriving hungry, naked, but true to instructions,
Docking on Earth, taking the one small step.

3.   BIRD PSALM

The Swallow said,
He comes like me,
Longed-for; unexpectedly.

The superficial eye
Will pass him by,
Said the Wren.

The best singer ever heard.
No one will take much notice,
Said the Blackbird.

The Owl said,
He is who, who is he
Who enters the heart as soft
As my soundless wings, as me.

4.   CHRISTMAS IN ENVELOPES

Monks are at it again, quaffing, carousing;
And stage-coaches, cantering straight out of Merrie England,
In a flurry of whips and fetlocks, sacks and Santas.

Raphael has been roped in, and Botticelli;
Experts predict a vintage year for Virgins.

From the theologically challenged, Richmond Bridge,
Giverny, a lugger by moonlight, doves. Ours

Costs less than these in money, more in time;
Like them, is hopelessly irrelevant,
But brings, like them, the eternal message

love